A FIRST LOOK AT THE WORLD OF PLANTS

By Millicent E. Selsam and Joyce Hunt
ILLUSTRATED BY HARRIETT SPRINGER

WALKER AND COMPANY ✹ NEW YORK

For Cameron

The authors wish to thank Dr. Howard S. Irwin, President of the New York Botanical Gardens, for checking the text of this book.

Text Copyright © 1978 by Millicent E. Selsam and Joyce Hunt
Illustrations Copyright © 1978 by Harriett Springer

First published in the United States of America in 1978 by the Walker Publishing Company, Inc.

Published simultaneously in Canada by Beaverbooks Limited, Pickering, Ontario

Trade ISBN: 0-8027-6298-0
Reinf. ISBN: 0-8027-6299-9

Library of Congress Catalog Card Number: 77-78088

Printed in the United States of America.

10 9 8 7 6 5 4 3 2 1

A *FIRST LOOK AT* SERIES

Each of the nature books for this series is planned to develop the child's powers of observation and give him or her a rudimentary grasp of scientific classification.

Any living thing that is not an animal is a plant.

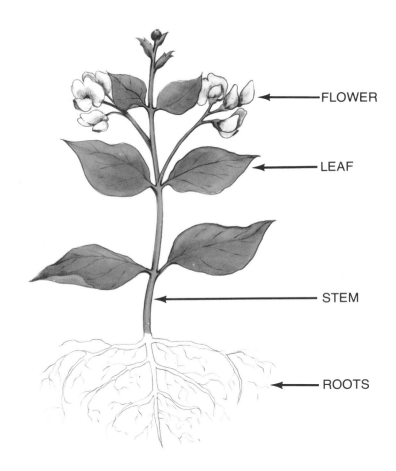

FLOWER

LEAF

STEM

ROOTS

When we think of a plant we usually think of
something that is green, has roots, stems, leaves, and flowers.

Here are some plants growing on the trunk of a tree.

Can you find roots, stems, leaves and flowers?
These plants have none and they are not green.

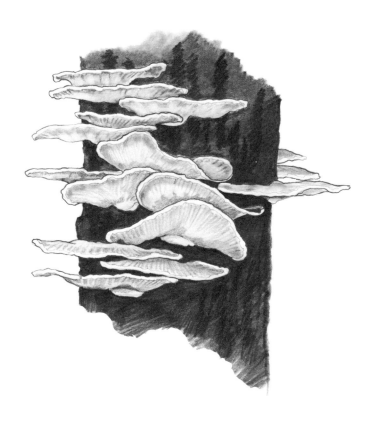

Here is another plant.
It is green and has roots, stems and leaves.
But can you find flowers?
This plant has none.

Plants are different.
Some have roots, stems and leaves.
Some do not.
Some have flowers.
Some do not.
Some are green.
Some are not.

Some plants are so big that a car can pass through them.

Some plants are so small that they can only be seen under a microscope.

There are some right on this page.
They are everywhere.
They are called bacteria.

BACTERIA (bak-TEE-ree-a)

Bacteria are the tiniest plants in the world.
Each plant is only a single cell.
A cell is the smallest unit of life.
Bacteria have only three shapes.
Some are round like tiny beads.
Some are shaped like chocolate sprinkles.
Some are twisted like tiny corkscrews.
Bacteria get their food from other plants and animals.

BACTERIA UNDER THE MICROSCOPE

ALGAE (AL-gee)

Some algae are almost as small as bacteria.
But they have chlorophyll (KLOR-o-fill).
Chlorophyll is green. Any plant that has
chlorophyll can make its own food.
Algae do not have roots, stems, leaves, or flowers.
Most of them live in water or in damp places on land.
Some, like the ones in this picture, are as tiny as dots.

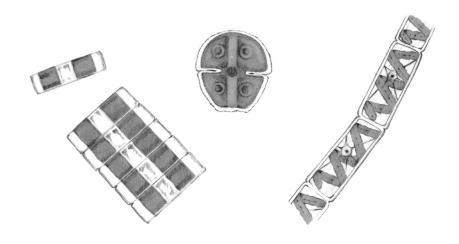

ALGAE UNDER THE MICROSCOPE

These tiny algae are found by the millions floating
on top of the sea as well as on lakes and ponds.
They are important because they are the basic food of
nearly all water animals.

Not all algae are tiny.
The seaweeds you find on the beach are algae too.
Match the seaweed to its name.

Sea Lettuce
Eyelash Seaweed
Palm Seaweed
Ribbon Seaweed
Mermaid's Wineglass

11

BRYOPHYTES (BRY-o-fites)

Liverworts and mosses are called bryophytes.
They do not live in water like most algae.
They are very small green plants that spread like
mats over damp ground.
They have no real roots, stems, or leaves
such as the bigger plants that live on land.
In bigger plants, water goes into the roots from the ground.
Then it travels through the stem in special tubes to the leaves.
In bryophytes, the whole plant is able
to soak up water when it rains.

There are two kinds of liverworts.
One kind looks like a single leaf.
The other kind looks like many leaves on a stem.
Which is which?

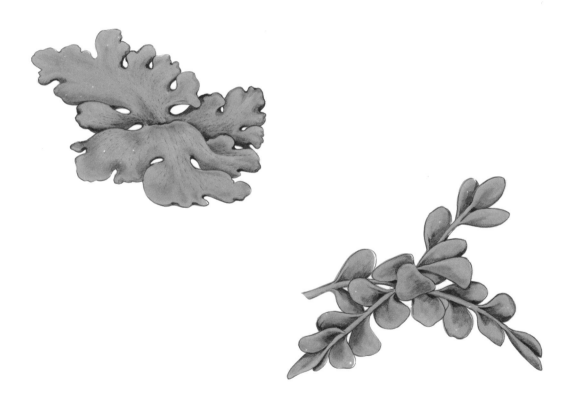

Both these liverworts grow flat on the ground.

Mosses are not flat on the ground.
They are usually a few inches above it.
In the spring and summer, mosses send up
little stalks with cases of spores.
Spores are as light as dust and can drift away
and form new plants just as seeds do.

TYPICAL MOSS

The spore cases have different shapes
and help us to tell mosses apart.

Find the spore case that looks like a hat with a long tassel.

Find the spore case that looks like a stringbean.

Find the spore case that looks like a pear.

Find the spore case that looks like an acorn.

Find the spore case that looks like a twisted candle.

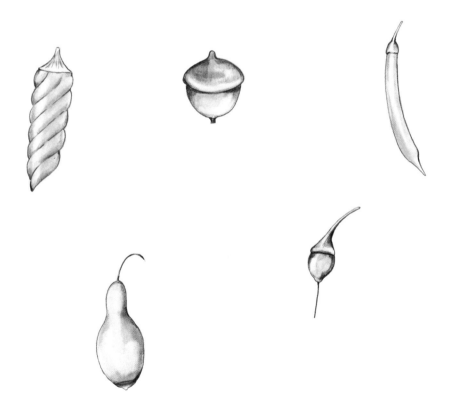

FUNGI (FUNJ-eye)

Fungi are not green like algae, liverworts, and mosses.
They are not one-celled like bacteria.
They have no roots, stems, or leaves.
The main part of a fungus (FUN-gus) is the network of threads under the ground or in wood.
These threads bring food and water to the rest of the plant.
Above the ground are the spore-making parts of the plant.

Mushrooms are a common type of fungus.

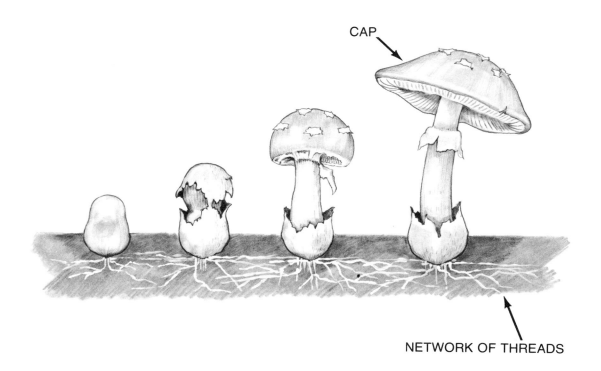

This is the way a mushroom grows.
Under the cap millions of spores are formed.

Mushrooms can be told apart by the shape of their caps.

Which mushroom looks like a table?

a bell?

an umbrella?

a flower?

Some fungi grow out of the trunks of trees and look
like little shelves. Because of this, they are called bracket fungi.
Threads grow into the wood and take food from it.
The spores come out from the underside of the bracket.

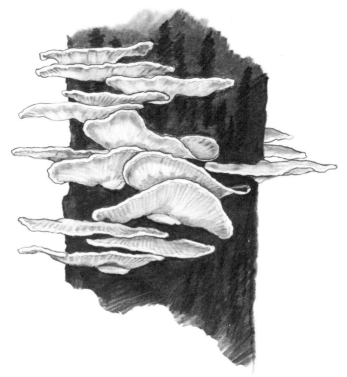

Puffballs are fungi that are round like balls.
When the balls ripen, the spores come puffing out like smoke.

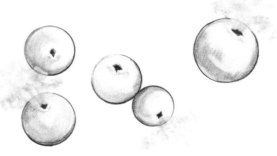

Molds are the fungi you see growing on bread, fruit, in
some cheese, and sometimes on the leather of your shoes.
Look for the mold with small, round, black spore cases.
Look for the mold that has branches at the tip.

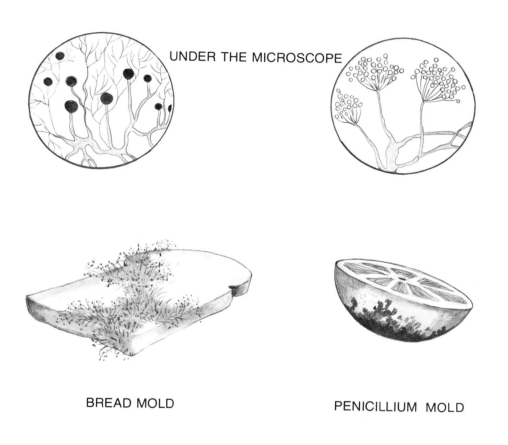

UNDER THE MICROSCOPE

BREAD MOLD

PENICILLIUM MOLD

Penicillium (pen-i-SIL-lee-um) is the mold
from which we get the medicine penicillin.

FERNS

Ferns do not live in water like most algae.
They are not low on the ground and do not soak up
water like mosses and liverworts.
They are larger green plants that live on land.
Ferns have real roots, underground stems, and leaves.
Their roots take in water, and the water travels
through the stem to the leaves.
Ferns form new plants from spores just as mosses and fungi do.

When a fern leaf comes up from the ground, it is tightly
curled like the end of a violin. Then it unfolds.

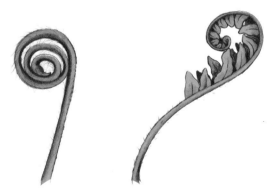

Many ferns have leaves that look
as though they were cut into smaller pieces.
They may seem to be cut only once.

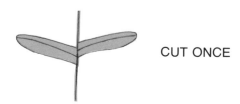

CUT ONCE

They may seem to be cut again into smaller pieces.

CUT TWICE

Then there are really lacy ferns where the leaves seem
to be cut three times into still smaller pieces.

CUT THREE TIMES

Ferns have spore cases in clusters on the undersides of the leaves.

Find the ones that look like kidney beans.

Find the ones that look like beads.

Find the ones that look like the links of a chain.

Find the ones that look like a long line
around the edge of the leaflets.

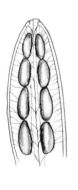

GYMNOSPERMS (JIM-no-sperms)

Gymnosperms have roots, stems, and leaves like ferns.
But they produce seeds instead of spores.
The word *gymnosperm* means "naked seed."
The seeds have no covering and can be found
between the scales of a cone.

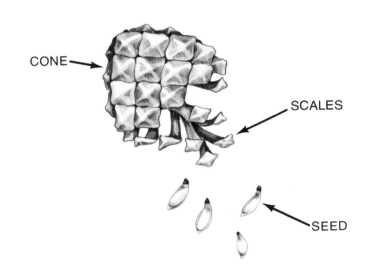

CONE

SCALES

SEED

Most gymnosperms are evergreen—they keep their leaves all winter.
They can be told apart by their leaves.
Pines have leaves like long, thin needles.
Firs have shorter needles.
Cedars have leaves like overlapping scales.
Which is which?

Cones also help us to tell gymnosperms apart.
Notice the different shapes.

Some are round like balls.

Some are long and narrow.

Some look like pineapples.

Some look like woody flowers.

ANGIOSPERMS (AN-gee-o-sperms)

Angiosperms are flowering plants.
They are different from gymnosperms in that their seeds
have a covering called a fruit.
To tell angiosperms apart, you have to look at leaves—

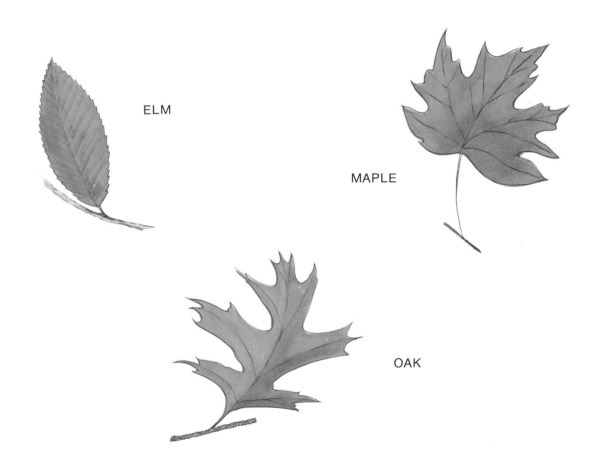

ELM

MAPLE

OAK

you have to look at flowers—

WILD HYACINTH

ROSE

BUTTERCUP

you have to look at fruits.

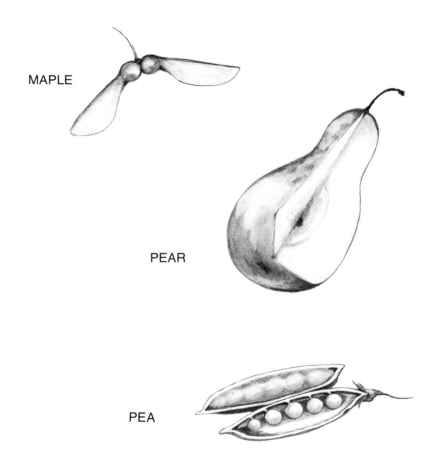

MAPLE

PEAR

PEA

Any part of a plant that has seeds in it is called a fruit.

THE WORLD OF PLANTS

Bacteria

Algae

Bryophytes

Fungi

Ferns

Gymnosperms

Angiosperms

32

J
581 S
SELSAM
  A FIRST LOOK AT THE WORLD OF
PLANTS
                    5.95